Red Undies
& Dutchman's Trousers

Red Undies

& Dutchman's Trousers

NAUGHTY PLANTS FOR EVERY OCCASION

SACHA LANGTON-GILKS

Collins

First published in 2007 by
Collins, an imprint of
HarperCollinsPublishers Ltd.
77–85 Fulham Palace Road
London
W6 8JB

The Collins website address is:
www.collins.co.uk

Collins is a registered trademark of HarperCollinsPublishers Ltd.

A catalogue record for this book is
available from the British Library.

ISBN-10 0-00-725890-9
ISBN-13 978-0-00-725890-1

Editorial Director: Jenny Heller
Copy Editor: Sarah Day
Assistant Editor: Kerenza Swift
Design and layout: Palimpsest Book Production Ltd, Stirlingshire
Illustrator: Xtina Lamb
Proofreader: Diana Vowles
Indexer: Sacha Langton-Gilks/Geraldine Beare

Set by Rowland Phototypesetting Ltd, Bury St Edmunds, Suffolk
Printed and bound by Printing Express, Hong Kong

Contents

Introduction 9

Naughty Plants 11
The Gay Boys' Border 25
The Religious Border 35
Posh Plants for Sun and Shade 43
Common Plants for Sun and Shade 51
The WAGs' Border 59
Plants to Give to People You Hate 67
Gardening Terms 75
Terribly Useful Garden Techniques 81
Garden Design Dissected 85

Appendix I 91
Appendix II 93
Acknowledgements 97
Index 99

I dedicate this tome to Esther Merton, my paternal grandmother, whose inimitable fingers were always in the sods. She is the only plantswoman who could have named a cultivar 'Sweaty Typist' *(Salvia* var. *turkestanica)*; its scent has also been compared to that of the male silver-backed gorilla.

Introduction

Dear Reader

Why do I garden? As a child, I was horticulturally abused by a family consisting entirely of gardeners, and I spent years resisting the magnetism of my plantswoman's pedigree. My glamorous parents deposited me in the usual emotionally bankrupt Anglican boarding school, where I scorned all instruction in the arts of cookery and flower-arranging. It was not until I had my own outside space that I succumbed to the family vice and allowed my genetic flair for plants and garden design to flourish.

This little book is the result of constant appeals by friends and fans for my favourite plants and planting tips based on my central gardening philosophy: right plant in the right place. For example, it is hopeless putting dry, religious plants like *Festuca glauca* 'Elijah Blue' in rich, moist soil crowded by naughty plants like unhygienic *Lobelia siphilitica*. If you plant with, rather than against, your conditions, you will have less work and healthier plants with no blood-pressure problems. By paying attention to the conditions in which the plants originate, you will soon find out with which other plants they best associate. Similarly, working with nature to control diseases by planting local, organic weeds to attract every known wildlife predator, buying in a few immigrant pests by mail and practising companion planting (*see*

Gardening Terms, p. 75) is much cheaper and more environmentally friendly than, if not as therapeutic as, spraying with lots of chemicals. Note: Do not take companion planting too far: marrying *Clematis* 'Prince Charles' and *Clematis* 'Princess Diana' does *not* work.

To help you attain a similarly thought-provoking range of plants to mine, I have named names *à la* Anna Pavord and selected key groups of plants which I have dipped into over the years. These groups have arisen from my constantly changing interests and moods, and those of my clients.

I first choose a planting style and select the group of plants I think would be right for the client and then adapt the list to the particular demands of the site. The plants are filed A–Z in the same way as is my adored handbook by darling Beth Chatto, with supplementary plant lists at the end of each group. For those interested in unlocking the key to good design, I have included a brief chapter revealing my insights, and two essential appendices unearth the secrets of my famous garden wardrobe and the menu at my exclusive garden café.

So, keep it *simplicifolia* and fingers crossed you too will end up *grandiflora*, *major* and *gloriosa*.

Yours faithfully
Sacha Langton-Gilks

Naughty Plants

As Dorothy Parker once quipped, 'You can lead a horticulture, but you can't make her think.' With this wonderful group of plants and my expert advice, you won't have to bother much either. Their versatility embraces the full range of conditions: full sun, part sun, soaking wet, partially wet, limp, unexciting, bored, frustrated, mischievous, under the weather, terminally ill, on good form or glowing. Be bold and liberal in their use and give your imagination free rein. For once, maintenance is not a chore but a positive boon – I have had relatively few face-lifts due to my intimacy with this inspirational group of plants.

For plants that are criminally naughty, however, *see* Plants to Give to People You Hate, p. 67.

All *Amorphophallus*

I think the more-phallus the merrier with regard to this very generously endowed genus of tuberous perennials, grown for their large and dramatic spathes. They produce only tiny flowers, but then nobody's perfect. The poor things are terribly frost-tender and like to be well appreciated and kept dry in the winter.

They are very happy to reproduce by seed in spring or

by offsets (*see* Gardening Terms, p. 78) in spring or summer, so you only have to worry about contraception in autumn and winter.

Bastard Balm *(Melittis melissophyllum)*

One of the family Labiatae, this plant is irresponsibly willing to propagate by seed, particularly in the autumn, and is so hardy that you will not be given the time of day the next morning. It is not quite such a problem in this socially deconstructed age but, if you live in the country and have old-school conservative parents, you may find it can still cause a lot of trouble.

Begonia 'Red Undies'

Thanks to Sue and Bleddyn at Crûg Farm for introducing me to this fabulous new line; they credit several bottles of red wine for the finishing touches.

Understandably, 'Red Undies' can only take a peep at the sun and prefers woodsy conditions, when it would probably be simpler to take them off altogether. If this perennial is happy, it will flower from July until the frosts, flaunting its blooms among the glorious foliage.

Clematis 'Horn of Plenty'

Sports a lovely rosy-mauve head and is surprisingly compact. If you are lucky, it can repeat while you are on holiday, in August, which is a must for those regularly interrupted by small children at the weekend.

All *Clitoria*

The neglect often suffered by this genus of perennials and evergreen climbing plants grown for their pea-like flowers is usually due to difficulty in locating them. The *RHS Plantfinder* can currently only find one supplier but says there were more a few years ago: this is odd, as they are not in short supply. The plant is *very* tender and *must* be overwintered indoors for protection. With the right fertile and well-drained conditions, it will reward persistent efforts with momentous results, such that your garden will never feel complete without it.

Usually propagate by seed in spring when sap is rising, having first gained suitable parental consent. If whitefly and red spider mite attacks occur, consult your doctor, and do not attempt biological controls by mail order.

All *Cnicus*

These variegated thistles are made for those who prefer large, rustic knickers to more practical undergarments. They are often used as summer bedding (*see* Gardening Terms, p. 79), although this could be considered rather uncomfortable. If you crave this kind of effect, perhaps you should seek out *Cnicus benedictus* for extra punishment (this works very well among the ascetics in a Religious Border. *See* p. 35).

All Cox Apples

I remain convinced that the Fall of Man must have been due to one of these sacred beauties. Despite centuries of strenuous effort by the Catholic church, these apples remain very popular and, although small, are all balls in the flavour department.

Good hygiene is extremely important if you wish to avoid pests and diseases, although I would urge caution if you are following the manuals which advocate spraying, as it is so difficult to get the timing right. In my inorganic days, I used to have to catch my husband when he was too inebriated to put up a coordinated struggle. So, in my considerable experience, an organic routine is more beneficial, which means selecting a healthy specimen from healthy stock and feeding it properly.

Dicentra spectabilis (Dutchman's Trousers)

It is so much fun to expose these gorgeous, naked white ladies in a spring border, and they go some way to explaining why Holland is the horticultural capital of the world. Dutch bedding displays have to be seen to be believed, particularly in Amsterdam. 'Dutchman's Trousers' look particularly lovely on dykes in a wild setting, something most men like the sound of.

Eryngium alpinum 'Superbum'

I'm sure I follow Roman practice when I place the emphasis on 'bum' and not on 'per'. I have often thought the Alps sound a little chilly – maybe that is why this cultivar is blue.

All *Gynura*

A genus with similar requirements to *Clitoria* (*see* p. 15) but with the added interest of attractive foliage and ease of propagation. Hence, even softwood will supply you with offspring, but probably only after you have been very nice. I reiterate the need for immaculate personal hygiene; otherwise, you could find yourself suffering from a nasty dose of smut.

Hedera helix 'Erecta' (Common English ivy)

Give *Hedera* 'Erecta' a chance, despite its undeservedly poor reputation for rampant growth. With imagination, this excellent cultivar can be trained to impressive heights; I've experienced enormous ones very successfully up against a wall. Maintenance can be an issue, especially when they get older, however these shortcomings are as nothing when compared to their near-universal appeal, which makes *Hedera* 'Erecta' just as effective as structural planting in a Gay Boys' Border (*see* p. 25).

Hoary Allison *(Berteroa incana)*

An introduced annual naturalised in wastegrounds like railway embankments but sometimes found in cultivated ground, if you know whom to ask. Posh hotel customer services are probably a good place to start, but only if you are discreet and generous.

Lobelia siphilitica

It goes without saying that this lovely plant, which originates from North America, is a skin- and eye-irritant and harmful if eaten. The Victorians took it to cure their secret affliction but, as we know, it didn't work.

Unsurprisingly, *siphilitica* likes moist conditions. Take great care with the companion planting for this plant and *never* put it near any *Gynura* (*see* p. 17).

Morning Glory *(e.g. Ipomoea hederacea)*

This lovely twining climber is half-hardy to frost-tender but is not even a perennial, which is hopeless and generates so much extra effort and stress. It needs to be brought inside in the winter to continue growing, which is understandable, unless you are the type to dip in Hampstead Pond on New Year's Day. For best results, give it a helping hand and talk dirty, as it needs lots of support; and then it will blossom beautifully and everyone will be happy.

Narcissus 'Canaliculatus'

A very rewarding variety once you have got your tongue around the tricky pronunciation. This popular daffodil is a sweetly scented tazzetta type but would be appreciated much more if used in large quantities, preferably spaced at regular intervals and planted at about a finger's depth. An isolated example looks ridiculous, with the added irritation that, having been introduced to such a marvellous thing, you would never want to stop at just one.

Nipplewort *(Lapsana communis)*

According to Richard Mabey, this English native is a 'common and rather lax annual of rough ground'. The name derives from the shape of its flower buds, which suggested to physicians such as the sixteenth-century Joachim Camerarius that they must be effective at healing ulcers of the nipples. I just tend to avoid ulcerous behaviour in that area.

The flowers have very sensible habits and take their bras off only on sunny mornings.

Orchis mascula (Early-purple orchid, Male orchid, Sweet ballocks, Dog-stones)

I am again indebted to Richard Mabey, and Geoffrey Grigson, for first-class naughty information on these beautiful native flowers. Apparently, in 1664, a certain Robert Turner suggested that there were enough of these orchids to pleasure all the seamen's wives in Rochester. You will, of course, appreciate that orchid means 'testicle' in Latin, as even a cursory glance at a picture of this plant shows. Therefore, herbalists from time immemorial enthusiastically pounded up the root as an (unsuccessful) aphrodisiac, and it was only boring Victorians like Ruskin who tried to hide such a shocking word-derivation with a politically correct substitute – wreathewort.

It goes without saying that a radical orchidectomy is a particularly extreme form of one-upmanship and is suitable only for the most masochistic garden obsessive.

Rosa 'Nathalie Nypels'

An extremely popular polyantha rose due to its health, its fragrance, its almost perpetual flowering and, due to a spreading growing habit which sadly happens to most of us at some time or other, its versatility.

Authorities on roses recommend this beauty in massed plantings, although I've never been much of a public naturist myself.

The open, upright clusters of flowers change with age from an appropriate mid-pink to almost white and are lightly cupped, thus obviating the need for under-wired support.

Try it up against a pillar with *Rosa* 'Buff Beauty' for knee-trembling effect.

Rosa 'Playboy'

Bred by Cocker in 1976, this rose has consistently repeated and has always been *very* popular as an exhibition Floribunda. The bling flowers are heavily styled – lightly double with wavy edges and handsome stamens. If you are not into older men, just avoid the ones that are redder, especially in hot weather. Having said that, 'Playboy', of any age, does at least last a long time on the bush.

I am reliably informed that this is an extremely rewarding rose, an opinion with which I am sure Hugh Heffner would agree. I am convinced that, had this exciting cultivar been available in the time of Emperor Heliogabalus (AD 204 – 222), he would have been sure to douse his guests with its petals, and none other, during his ill-fated orgy, during which a vast quantity of petals cascaded down from the imperial ceilings, smothering the fortunates beneath.

Scrophularia nodosa (Knotted figwort, Throatwort)

Culpeper writes of this unhygienic plant that it 'dissolves clotted & congealed blood within the body, coming by any wounds, bruise or fall; and is effectual for any kernels, bunches or wens growing in the flesh, and for the piles'. It is also effective against scrofula, 'the king's evil', a useful quality in a wicked plant.

'Fig' is an old word for piles, which both the globular red flower-buds and the root protuberances were thought to resemble. I have never thought to check this myself.

I recommend strict personal hygiene when planting this native – and do keep it away from *Hedera helix* 'Erecta' and *Lobelia siphilitica* (*see* pp. 17 and 18).

Sisyrinchium 'E. K. Balls'

Does very well in full sun but obviously hates to spend any time sitting in water during the winter without a dry-suit, or else a nasty case of rot beckons.

Looks are deceptive, as the rather genteel, lovely, violet-blue flowers of this plant in fact have the balls to self-seed prolifically around the garden, which, for those gardeners who don't like it *roughii*, can cause a great deal of extra maintenance.

Sticky Willy *(Galium aparine)*

This is a scrambling annual that can grow ten foot in a season (perhaps plastic surgeons should investigate the biochemistry of this plant for more natural and less invasive 'tips' for the under-endowed). Fascinated children still pick this vigorous native to stick on to each other's coats and hair because of its coating of hooked bristles, which make it difficult to detach. This gives rise to its many names, from 'cleavers' to 'kisses'. For those of us who were isolated in a girls' boarding school, it will always be a delicious bun lovingly coated in sticky white icing.

Willy Lily *(Arum maculatum)*

Other common names for this plant are parson's billycock, cuckoo-pint (short for pintle or penis) and dog's cock. In fact, Geoffrey Grigson records about 90 different local tags, of which my favourite is Kitty-come-down-the-lane-jump-up-and-kiss-me. The killjoy Victorians were probably responsible for the polite name cuckoo-flower, which seems hypocritical given that they used the roots as a 'stiffening' agent. The trouble all stems from the phallic shape of the pale green sheath, sometimes blushed purple, hooding the spadix. In some areas, before a young man went out in the evening, he would place a cuckoo-pint in his shoe, after the saying: 'I place you in my shoe, let all girls be drawn to you.' These days they try to drive a big car.

Naughty Supplements

Aster 'Climax'

Aster oblongifolius 'Fanny's'

Astilbe 'Bumalda'

Bum-pipe ('dandelion' in Banffshire)

Cock's Head (*Plantago lanceolata*)

Dahlia 'Furka'

Ginkgo biloba 'Tit'

Hemerocallis 'Little Bugger'

Hemerocallis 'Lusty Leland'

Magnolia 'Hot Lips'

Magnolia 'Randy'

Malus domestica 'Golden Knob'

Malus domestica 'Lady's Finger'

Naked Ladies, Naked Nannies, Naked Boys, Naked Virgins *(Colchicum autumnale)*

Phlox adsurgens 'Red Buttes'

Prunus domestica 'Warwickshire Drooper'

Pussy Willow *(Salix caprea)*

Welsh Dicks *(Salix purpurea)*

The Gay Boys' Border

T his group of plants, while not traditional, is becoming increasingly high profile and will inject some serious talent, even theatricality and flair, into your garden design. It is one of my favourites. Restraint is not one's guide here, but these plants do combine particularly well with Religious plants (*see* p. 35), sharing a love of rich conditions, while they have also gained notoriety for their irreverent coupling in particular sections of the cottage garden.

Look particularly for plants with the suffixes *erecta*, *rigidus*, *camporum*, *alternifolia*, *recta*, *gayanum*, some *hirsutum* and cultivars named 'The Queen' in any language. Absolutely avoid those with *confusa*, *flaccida* and *pendula*, which can be such a let-down. Half-hardy plants are often a disappointment too, I find. If you follow these simple little rules you'll learn to identify the best specimens with ease, as they often display double flowers, bright colours and exotic foliage. Don't be frightened by them: double hybrids tend not to cross-pollinate, so you will not have the problem of messy, rampant seeding all over the place.

Notes:

a) If you are a purist, select only male clones of dioecious plants for total horticultural homosexuality

b) I have not yet fully got to grips with Nicholas Harberd's thriller decoding the genome of thale cress, but for the purposes of this chapter I can divulge that this frisky weed has both GAI and gai genes which hang out at DELLAS. This select club is dominated by the gai group, who punch well above their weight by conferring dwarfism over the GAI set. So, for a wild gay border, just let that cress run amok.

Azalea (*Rhododendron*) 'Adonis'

For the gay classicist with lime-free soil and a sheltered spot, this gorgeous, small but perfectly formed evergreen shrub has deliciously compact white flowers with frilly margins, hose-in-hose (one flower within another rather than a Tudor description of homosexual behaviour). You could also try *Azalea* 'Queen Wilhelmina' if you are after a vermilion red or *Azalea* 'Willy' for the perfect fleshy soft pink.

Campsis radicans 'Flamenco'

This deciduous climber gives a bravura performance, which suits the more artistic and theatrical clients in this group. Like them, however, it is slightly tender and should therefore be given a sheltered, sunny site for the best chance of survival through a cold winter. The effort will be worthwhile for the bright orange-red trumpets that proliferate in August. It will be more widely grown as our climate continues to warm, a situation which will then reflect its present massive success in Brighton.

Cercis canadensis 'Forest Pansy'

This stunning small tree is a perfect feature for a small town garden, even though it probably prefers to frequent the sylvan glades of Clapham Common. It has fashionable rounded purple leaves with pink flowers on bare stems in late spring, and a top garden designer has it in splendid isolation in a pot on the terrace.

Clematis 'Princess Diana'

This plant has iconic status in this border, and she can be grown through early flowering shrubs, if space is at a premium, where her heartbreaking, tragic pink flowers will continue to captivate up to the end of September.

Dianthus 'Gran's Favourite'

A very cherished member of this border, which always outlives impulse buys. It always associates well with *Rosa* 'Mother's Day'.

Fagus sylvatica 'Pendula'

I know I told you at the beginning of the chapter to avoid anything *pendula*, as endless weeping can be very tiresome, but I think you will agree that this tree deserves to be exempt. *The Hillier Manual of Trees and Shrubs* describe it as spectacular, and the venerable authority W.J. Bean gives an enticing description of unevenly undulated veins with a hairy midrib (especially underneath). Unusually, the nuts are triangular and a disappointing ⅝ of an inch long, but at least they are normally in a pair. Getting to them is obviously difficult as they are encased in a bristly, hard, fore-lobed husk – maybe it's simpler to just leave it on.

Phormium 'Rainbow Queen'

This New Zealand flax instantly injects the exotic quality of *Priscilla, Queen of the Desert* into your border, and the particularly striking foliage of this cultivar, bronze-green with rose-red stripes, makes it a classic. It is infinitely preferable to the rather sickly soft-yellow leaves flushed with apricot of its partner *Phormium* 'Apricot Queen'.

Phygelius x rectus 'African Queen'

The perfect small shrub for this border, this Cape-figwort will tolerate most soil conditions, although it does need some shelter, especially from behind. It has masses of red tubular flowers in summer.

Rhododendron 'Faggetter's Favourite'

This marvellous evergreen, brought to you straight from the racy pages of *Hillier's Manual*, was raised by W. C. Slocock of Woking, who must have exhibited good staying power to have succeeded in an area with such stiff competition. A tall grower, it has fine foliage and large trusses of sweetly scented shell-pink flowers.

Rhododendron 'Kokinshita'

Not everyone's preferred choice. *Hillier's* instructs one to '*see under* Evergreen Azaleas', where you will not find nearly enough interesting detail about this deviant hybrid which originated in Southern Japan but was later developed in Belgium, England, France and Germany. These large funnel-shaped flower types are particularly popular at Christmas, when they are forced. This tender plant will produce deepest satisfaction when given proper protection and planted in a thoroughly prepared hole.

Rosa 'Camp David'

This is a hybrid tea rose (*see* Gardening Terms, p. 77) bred in Germany in 1984 but never actually introduced there. Instead, according to the specialists, it has been a roaring success in Australia, where it is much appreciated at exhibitions and obviously fits in well with the outdoor, body-beautiful beach culture.

It is a healthy rose, excellent for cutting, although this is a practice of which I approve only *after* a trip to the psychiatrist.

Rosa 'Dolly Parton'

This iconic rose was raised in the US from parents 'Duftwolke' and 'Oklahoma'. A strong, sweet scent emanates from very bright, buxom flowers, which are difficult to blend with others but are excellent value in the vase. Her enormous popularity, particularly in the US, stems partially from the fact that she has had to struggle with a harsh upbringing and a documented susceptibility to mildew and black spot, which means that there now exist healthier roses in this luminescent scarlet. This does not seem to have dented her legendary status in this border.

Rosa 'The Fairy'

This darling rose was bred in 1932 from, appropriately, 'Paul Crampel' and 'Lady Gay'. It is the world's most popular and widely grown Polyantha. I think this possibly stems from its exciting, naturally loose habit allied to a frilly, ruffled appearance that comes from the flowers being held in long, airy clusters. It is marvellously easy to grow and roots quickly, something some people still struggle to come to terms with, especially in the country. Its other key advantage is the ability to withstand disease – its vigour remains undimmed and symptoms like nasty blackspot can safely be ignored.

There is also the frisson of being able to choose a darker sport in a much deeper pink, known as 'Lovely Fairy', introduced by the Dutch (famously liberal in these matters).

Trachelospermum (all cultivars)

This must-have oriental evergreen climber will add year-round excitement to your life. Try to give it some support for the first few years, by which time, if it doesn't irritate you, it should have learned how to be self-clinging. The tiny creamy-white flowers in summer exude a fantastic scent but definitely need a hot wall for their most enjoyable performance.

Reinforcements

Campanula lactiflora 'Pouffe'
Dahlia 'Gay Princess'
Hemerocallis 'Gay Rapture'
Hemerocallis 'Tonia Gay'
Iris spuria subs. musselmanica
Lamium maculatum 'White Nancy'
Penstemon whippleanus
Rosa 'Lagerfeld'
Rosa 'La Reine'
Viola tricolor (Wild pansy)
Yucca flaccida 'Golden Sword'

The Religious Border

This border is not for the low-maintenance gardeners among us, requiring, as it does, a significant level of commitment, discipline and blind faith. Even I have to confess that the sight of this border can instinctively bring on a rush of guilt. Thou shalt tie up the roses and train them so that they may blossom into flowering pillars of rectitude. Thou shalt also ruthlessly excommunicate bishop's weed wheresoever it may be found, and thou shalt not allow any feelings of weakness or greed inspired by the pretty flowers and tempting young green shoots in spring.

Historically, these plants have associated well with those in the Gay Boys' Border and have often performed to the highest level in rich, retentive soil – except for the ascetic *Festuca*, which continues to prick the conscience of the Roses of the Vatican and the episcopal *Dahlia* in its relentless search for the poor but pure conditions of the original disciples. Pray for all plants with the Latin suffixes *benedictus*, *magdalene*, *prostratus* and, probably, *misera*.

Bishop's Weed (*Aegopodium podagraria*; Devil's guts, Ground-elder)

This perennial, thought of as a total pest by gardeners, was possibly introduced by the Romans as medicine against gout.

It is excellent cooked as spinach and served with butter but technically can be allowed only in a wilderness setting – 40 days and nights with nothing but locusts and wild honey.

Caryopteris x Clandonensis 'Heavenly Blue'

This deciduous sub-shrub provides a welcome calm 'zen' to a potentially overwrought border, as well as a cool contrast to the hot-headed, high-church cardinals and bishops elsewhere in the Religious Border. It forms an upright mass of grey-green leaves and tubular blue flowers in late summer, which chime very well with the evergreen *Camellia x Williamsii* 'Bow Bells'.

Dahlia 'Bishops of . . . Canterbury, Lancaster, Leicester, Llandaff, York and Auckland'

This convocation of high-profile ecclesiastics is currently very fashionable in hot borders, which must prove rather uncomfortable. They all have brightly coloured flowers, which have little to do with bishop's purple (except for Leicester), with either bronze or chocolate-coloured leaves. They have always performed better in rich conditions, requiring regular feeding, although, traditionally, blood and bonemeal was avoided on a Friday. If you are worried, just pray and genuflect, genuflect, genuflect.

Erigeron 'Quakeress'

This plant gives something a little odd to add some doctrinal tension to the border. It may not speak until the spirit moves it, but this clump-forming perennial does have dark lilac-pink daisy-like flowers throughout the summer.

Festuca glauca 'Elijah Blue' (Blue fescue)

This drier character comes from a group of evergreen, tuft-forming, perennial grasses.

It looks very out of place and uncomfortable among the high-ranking church officials and should instead be placed in a large congregation of its own, which would naturally include individuals like *Carex stricta*, *Carex flagellifera and Rosmarinus prostratus*.

Linaria purpurea 'Canon Went' (Toadflax)

This appropriately erect, slender perennial bears lovely violet-purple flowers from early summer to autumn but only self-seeds true if isolated from the species, which probably condemns this sociable plant to a great deal of soul-searching.

Magnolia macrophylla 'Holy Grail'

The *macrophylla* varieties, according to *Hillier's Manual*, are awe-inspiring small trees when seen alone in their grandeur. This particularly sought-after variety is naturally a superior form which is not widely distributed to the masses; this only adds to its allure.

Our Lady's Thistle, Holy Thistle or Milk Thistle *(Silybum marianum)*

Obviously introduced by an anxious pagan Roman propaganda department which thought that suggesting Mary had a sily [sic] bum which prickles would warn budding Christians that the Immaculate Conception was not fortuitous. Mary had the last laugh, however, as this very pretty fresh-green and white variegated annual with rose-purple flowers seeds itself with abandon, even on biblical stony ground.

Rosa 'Cardinal Hume'

This rose behaves in a strong and reliable manner, is unwavering in its habit and therefore does not need to be kept in a cold frame to sustain its faith during winter, unlike *Lobelia cardinalis*. It has complicated ancestry involving a Californian but fortunately has managed to resist further breeding. The correct crimson flowers have an unexpectedly spicy scent but are followed by worryingly glowing scarlet hips.

Rosa 'The Prioress'

'The Prioress' has the very strange parentage of 'Ma Perkins' and 'Madame Pierre Oger'. She has a moderate but fruity scent, repeats, which is a little harsh for her congregation, and sensibly grows much better in hot climates. Luckily, she is usually healthy and goes about her heavenly duties with zeal, but at close encounter she can come across as stiff and prickly. Nevertheless, even in our secular age, this English rose still attracts followers.

Note: The Reverend Joseph Pemberton raised some stupendous hybrid musks in his Essex garden in the 1920s, including *Rosa* 'Felicia'. The reverend was a very keen amateur rosarian, which does seem a trifle odd for an Anglican churchman.

Further Blessings

Aster novi-belgii 'Archbishop'; there are also
deacons, choirboys and a sexton
Aster ericoides 'Rosy Veil'
Ceanothus thyrsiflorus 'Borne Again'
Fuchsia 'Requiem'
Hemerocallis 'Twenty Third Psalm'
Iris sibirica 'Harpswell Hallelujah'
Magnolia 'Heaven Scent'
Malus domestica 'Ten Commandments'
Malus domestica 'Reverend W. Wilks'
Rosa 'The Friar'

Posh Plants for
Sun and Shade

To give the effect of generations of breeding and true haughtycultural class in your garden, the following plants are excellent. These plants best suit classic-style gardens and can be ruined by inappropriate planting (*see* Common Plants, p. 51). This docs not mean to say that they are not versatile; Posh Plants are often successful in association with Naughty Plants and, although it would be unusual now, historically, youngest sons often discovered their vocation in the Religious Border. These days, the situation is more fluid, as those rich enough have even been known to socialise with WAGs, especially at charity events, but partnerships are usually short term.

If you decide to choose your own posh plants – something I do not recommend – then be sure to pay strict attention to the plant's social provenance and check that it has a bona fide title. Examples of the minefield into which you are entering are *Rosa* 'Lady Waterlow' and *Rosa* 'Lady Mary Fitzwilliam'. The former is an example of a social climber, something you *must* try to avoid if you want to achieve a seamless example of posh planting. This rose will climb five metres in the climes of California, where, doubtless, they turn a blind eye to a less than perfect bloodline. Here in England she struggles to attain even two metres, reflecting her less than auspicious origins. The latter is even worse: an impostor. The upper classes have, however, always had a reputation for welcoming the odd self-made self-publicist into their echelons, if she is talented enough.

I have tended to avoid plants with foreign titles, as this is a specialist area and there appear to be far too many of them. Foreign sovereigns are acceptable, though, such as *Rosa* 'Queen of Denmark'. Those with spurious titles, such as *Lupinus* 'The Chataleine', which is obviously a plant on the make, must be avoided. The same can be said for plants which try to suggest class, such as *Iris* 'Champagne Elegance', which would be better off in a WAGs' Border.

If you are confused, buy a copy of *Debrett's Peerage* and stick to the following Latin suffixes only: *nobilis* and *regale* (for example, *Laurus nobilis*, *Lilium regale* and *Osmunda regalis*). You cannot possibly have too many of these.

His Royal Highness The Prince of Wales holds the National Collection of *Hosta* at Highgrove, which means that you can use any *Hosta* and do not have to stick to 'Royal Splendour' and 'Royal Standard'. Even the marvellous, glaucous foliage of *Hosta* 'Big Daddy' can be indulged in shady areas.

Clematis 'Princess Diana'

One of the late-flowering types, with tulip-shaped flowers from July to September in pale pink with a pink central bar. I find this a little overwrought in colour, a little too attention-seeking, so I tend to recommend the classic white 'Duchess of Edinburgh' instead. However, for some clients, their devotion to the memory of this style icon involves designing a horticultural shrine to her memory. This obviously also includes the funereal white rose 'Princess of Wales', which the late Princess herself chose to raise money for charity. Tragically, commentators have noted, in its native England it is a martyr to blackspot and, when faced with inclement conditions, its flowers crush in the rain.

Clematis 'Prince Charles'

His Royal Highness has a long flowering season, like many in his family. The compact, mauve-blue-blooded flowers from June to September represent excellent value for tax-payers' money and are reliably hardy, a useful quality in a future monarch. Do try to respect the organic principles behind his success – spraying with anything other than Ecover washing-up liquid would be tantamount to treason.

Ilex x altaclerensis 'Golden King'

This holly will happily live in industrial conditions or by the sea and is said to be one of the best golden-variegated hollies. Any reversions in the foliage must be cut out *immediately*, or your monarch will abdicate its golden title and become a green commoner. Inappropriately, this holly is a female clone, but sexual orientation in horticulture is a *very* complicated subject. For more information I refer you to Wilfrid Blunt's biography of Carl Linnaeus, whom he refers to as our 'foremost botanical pornographer'.

Rosa 'The Queen Elizabeth'

The apogee of this border, this tough rose naturally thrives in England, where its lovely petals are unaffected by rain. Its fair constitution means that in hot climates, the pink flowers fade without a sensible hat, but they keep their colour well elsewhere. *Rosa* 'The Queen Elizabeth' has a narrow and upright habit, as you would expect from a Windsor, is disease-resistant, vigorous and will even grow well in poor soil. This popular rose has a good sweet scent and repeats very well. The climbing variety is even more popular, but this sort of behaviour should be discouraged, as it is deeply undignified for a monarch.

Rosa 'Queen Mother'

Portly reference books on roses always stress the reliability and popularity of this stalwart. This has been the most widely sold rose in England, along with mugs and figurines for the mantelpiece, which somewhat diminishes its snob appeal. Nevertheless, it epitomises the establishment and beautifully demonstrates the flair of the late Queen Mother for communicating with the masses.

Rosa 'Lady Hillingdon'

Although there are countless grander titles, classy wit has always fared well, especially when it's a trifle naughty, and I therefore always include this delightful rose. Born posh, the Hon. Alice Marion Harbord (1857–1940) is famous for the following aphorism:'I am happy to know that Charles calls on my bedchamber less frequently than of old. As it is, I endure but two calls a week and when I hear his steps outside my door I lie down on my bed, close my eyes, open my legs and *think of England.*'

Her rose is one of the loveliest in its colour range of the tea roses, a soft apricot which contrasts beautifully with the crimson emerging foliage. It perfectly exemplifies the acceptable face of upward mobility and elevation through the upper echelons of society.

Acceptable Addenda

Sun

Aster amellus 'King George'
Chrysanthemum 'Duchess of Edinburgh'
Cotinus coggygria 'Royal Purple'
Crocosmia x crocosmiiflora 'Lady Hamilton'
Geum 'Lady Stratheden'
Hemerocallis 'Siloam Rose Queen'
Hemerocallis 'Siloam Royal Prince'
Iris laevigata 'Regal'
Paeonia lactiflora 'Duchesse de Nemours'
Potentilla thurberi 'Monarch's Velvet'
Rosa 'Queen of Denmark'

Shade

Galanthus 'Lady Beatrix Stanley'
Geranium x oxonianum 'Lady Moore'
Helleborus x hybridus 'Lady Charlotte Bonham-Carter'
Heuchera 'Lady Romney'
The King Fern *(Dryopteris affinis* 'Cristata'*)*

Common Plants for Sun and Shade

This chapter is firmly aimed at those aspiring to a classy ladies-who-lunch-and-do-afternoon-classes-in-garden-design-in-Chelsea border. This sort of lady needs to know what to avoid, otherwise she will fall foul of the Haughtycultural Taste Police. These terrifying garden critics can reduce even the most confident gardener to a gibbering wreck with one comment. A general rule of thumb is to steer clear of all plants with suffixes *vulgare*, *officinalis and hookeriana.*

Having been exposed to such a plethora of planting styles as a child, I seem to have bypassed the intricacies of the British Horticultural class system and, as a result, I have what some might say are suspiciously wide-ranging garden tastes. I have a weakness for pub hanging baskets in garish colours and cheerful seaside-town bedding schemes, and I find miniature conifer gardens in the suburbs just as fascinating as Tom Stuart-Smith's latest designs. Some of you will be reading with horrified speed at this point. But if you're one of those Howard Stern Shock-Tactics gardeners aiming at a Jeff Koons postmodern style, then these might be just the plants for you. Just ignore the snobbish remarks.

Aquilegia vulgaris var. *Stellata* 'Nora Barlow'

A lethal combination of an unfortunate suffix and the unfashionable end of television. This is an unstylish plant with fully double flowers in red on green. If you really feel the need for spring colour, try *Primula allionii* 'Mary Berry' for a more unusual plant which will keep the Joneses guessing.

Astrantia major 'Sunningdale Variegated'

A nasty suburban experiment with white and green variegated leaves accompanying pink-tinged, greenish-white flowers, which looks as if it is trying too hard. A style write-off. Remember South Fork at its most excessive and merge it with stockbroker Surrey – a nightmare of faux-respectable garden style.

Chrysanthemum x superbum 'Wirral Supreme'

This cultivar of the Shasta daisy is a double with short, central florets. The foliage is the usual coarse, lobed, toothed leaves. The combination of geography and soubriquet is hideous.

Clematis 'Belle of Woking'

Another oxymoron. This is one of the late-flowering clematis that can be grown through spring-flowering shrubs, if you need your plants to work hard to earn their space. This cultivar has double silvery-mauve flowers in June and July. I always think the use of mauve can betray a distinct lack of breeding, and the double flowers only compound the effect. Other ones to avoid are 'Lemon Chiffon', 'Ramona', 'Gipsy Queen' and the *montana* 'Marjorie' and 'Mayleen'.

Hemerocallis 'Pardon Me'

Guaranteed to cause deep discomfort, this vulgar day-lily is red with a yellow throat and it 'repeats' from May to September. Horrible. The only solution is to water it with Gaviscon until it 'repeats' no more.

Malus domestica 'Brown Nose'

This self-fertile cider apple is perfect for the up-and-coming gardener from Hereford with a particular interest in historic orchards and no qualms about immersing themselves in quantities of manure. All this pushiness results in a quantity of juice of a medium, bittersweet flavour.

Miscanthus sinensis 'Gnome'

This dwarf form has pink flower plumes which will look good all winter. Due to their unfortunate association with the mass-produced figurines, however, this easy-to-grow plant cannot be used in a garden aspiring to any kind of stylistic merit and would make it an easy target for the Garden Critics.

Rosa 'Mrs Honey Dyson'

The bizarre association of the successful domestic appliance and the name often given to golden retrievers/labradors has in fact produced a lovely rose which the cognoscenti at Hadspen, the marvellous Nori and Sandra Pope, have used effectively against the wall in the peach border. Nevertheless, for the aspirant haughtyculturalist this rose is much too difficult to place and it should only be attempted by the *crème de la crème*.

Tulipa 'Maureen', 'Shirley' and 'Wendy Love'

Any tulip grower using a description in a catalogue such as 'unusual, but very attractive' is relying on estate agent parlance to try to shift something ghastly. There are some truly horrendous tulips out there – the early, double-flowered 'Abba' is an eye-popping, lacquer-red which could only safely be planted in glorious isolation on stage.

'Angélique' calls itself peony-flowered which is, in itself, very pushy for a common pink tulip.

If you are worried, chose a species. It is true that a few of these still offer pitfalls for the unwary or novice gardener anxious to present a classy selection, for example, *Tulipa clusiana* 'Cynthia', but they will at least indicate to the Right Sort of Gardener a favourable general direction.

Appropriate Addenda

Sun

Delphinium 'Yvonne'

Dianthus 'Doris'

Geum 'Mrs J. Bradshaw'

Paeonia lactiflora 'Barrymore'

Verbascum 'Jackie'

Zantedeschia 'Kiwi Blush'

Shade

Astilbe 'Gloria'

Fuchsia 'Phyllis'

Fuchsia 'Tracie Ann'

Heuchera 'Chocolate Ruffles'

Iris 'Pauline' (Reticulata)

The WAGs' Border

Designing gardens for recently self-made super-wealthy clients, many of whom have self-built homes, involves a strong focus on celebrating their new-found wealth and celebrity status. Your job is primarily to pander to the media-driven desires of the Wives and Girlfriends.

Swimming pools – with all the extras – feature large, along with hot tubs, barbecues, cinemas, designer lighting, five-car garages, tennis courts and impregnable security.

The following plants have worked very well with these features; just don't expect the traditionally conservative Garden Critics to give you glowing reviews at any charity open days your clients organise.

You can include some of the Common Plants, as similar characteristics apply, but use with discretion. As a general rule, seek out a more flashy plant that favours non-retentive soil, a *substantial* maintenance schedule and the Latin suffixes *lurida*, *grande*, *monieri*, *fortunei* and *megaphyllum*.

Elements of this new style are now becoming increasingly popular and attracting widespread media coverage, although it is true to say that, due to their reliance on gadgets, these gardens can date very quickly, so you must make sure that your client has enough cash to upgrade whenever necessary.

Bergenia 'Baby Doll'

This hybrid of these versatile evergreen plants should be very at home here with its dwarf habit and soft-pink flowers in the spring. It is as tough as a set of hair extensions and will cope with conditions ranging from blazing poolside to stadium shade.

Crocosmia x crocosmiiflora 'Zeal Tan'

A classic plant for this border, with brash, outward-facing, big, deep-red flowers in late summer after a long spell on the Sunseeker. Think the very latest shade of juicy lip colour.

Helenium 'Chelsey'

The Americanisation of the spelling says it all. This daisy-type perennial is crimson with yellow flecks, but it can flop in very rich conditions, unlike certain footballers' girlfriends, and will then need support. These plants are becoming increasingly common in modern borders and as such are widely photographed (*see OK, Hello, Heat* and *Titbits*).

Heuchera 'Red Spangles'

A genus of evergreen, summer-flowering perennials which are the Versace and Gucci of the plant world, heucheras all have designer names and describe clumps of leaves that are usually tinted the latest self-tan bronze, or purple, and often have totally superfluous frills. This particular example has lasting bright red flowers and untypical green leaves. Other favourites are *H. americana* 'Beauty Colour' and 'Obsidian'.

Lobelia 'Tania'

This plant has pretensions to middle-class respectability, and its crimson-purple flowers contrast with green leaves marbled pink to give the extra splash of colour so beloved of this type of gardener. This perennial does not appreciate drying out in the summer but will tolerate being watered with a magnum of vintage Bollinger during hosepipe bans.

Try 'Tania' with lilies 'Destiny' and 'Cheyenne', *Hemerocallis* 'Anastasia', *Camellia japonica* 'Tiffany' and any of the *Lathyrus* 'Jet Set Group'.

Papaver orientale 'Brooklyn'

This oriental poppy has been specifically bred for foliage that lasts throughout the season and a ruby-red flower that often re-blooms. It may revert to a more conventional name in adolescence to avoid the glare of the paparazzi but, in my experience, this is seldom the case, and they usually go on to breed even flashier cultivars, which flower earlier and earlier. This poppy works very well with *Pelargonium* 'Romeo'.

Rosa 'Bobby Charlton'

A legend in this type of scheme, peerless in its class, with lots of awards, this lovely deep-pink rose has a good sweet scent, is a vigorous performer with strapping great leaves and responds wonderfully to good management. Unfortunately for a footballer, blackspot is often a problem later in the season, so a substitute should always be available — or an excellent beautician.

Rosa 'Fame'

Absolutely indispensable in this setting, this Grandiflora rose, bred in the US, has cherry-pink flowers that repeat well (which the clients *love*) and a light scent. This is the acceptable face of modern celebrity, not seeking notoriety but a badge to the stewards' enclosure at Henley or the members' tent at the Cartier Polo.

This rose tends to associate with the vigorous and quite outsized *Rosa* 'Celebrity', which, unfortunately for the paparazzi, has large hooked prickles, and also with *Rosa* 'Super Star'. The latter was a sensation when first introduced in the US, because of its surgically enhanced pigmentation, but was later eclipsed by more low-maintenance roses, due to an unfortunate susceptibility to disease. It is still happy in Mediterranean climates however.

Good substitutions

Hemerocallis 'Blonde is Beautiful'

Hemerocallis 'Eighteen Carat'

Hosta 'Stiletto' and 'Tattoo'

Hydrangea Sprrata 'Tiara'

Iris sibirica 'Super Ego'

Lilium 'Crystal Palace'

Lupinus 'Aston Villa'

Nymphaea 'Pink Starlet'

Potentilla fruticosa 'Chelsea Star'

Rosa 'Champagne Cocktail', 'Climbing Fashion', 'Pur Caprice', 'Sunseeker', 'Wembley Stadium' and 'Weightwatcher's Success'

Rhododendron vernicosum 'McLaren T71'

Tulipa 'Monte Carlo'

Viola cazorlensis 'Colleen'

Plants to Give to People You Hate

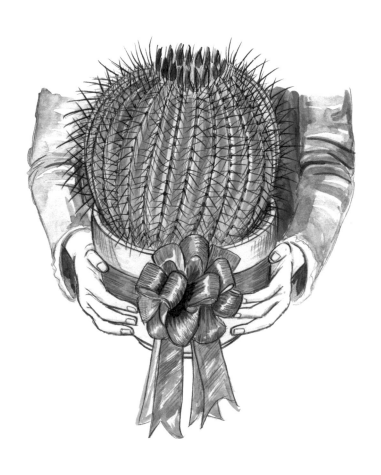

Unfortunately, due to the scale of my professional horticultural success and an opinionated and fast tongue, I have made enemies in my busy life and have, on occasion, resorted to underhand measures to wreak revenge. As my enemies are all gardeners of one type or another, I think the plants below are the perfect tools for retribution.

It is worth expending considerable effort planning your gift to ensure you reap maximum returns. Think carefully about the prospective position in your enemy's garden and the uses to which the plants might be put. Be very sure that your gift cannot rebound on you. Where appropriate, suggest that your gift was recommended by a very good nursery, so that you yourself are not in the frame.

Cannabis sativa (Pot, Hash, Weed)

I find this naughty plant an invaluable tool in the fight against the inevitable aches and pains that ensue from passionate gardening, but also a first-class weapon in the frontline battle which is Best in Show at the floral tent of the village fête. In my experience, a large, moist special brownie at teatime works wonders when delivered, via a

WI go-between, to a particularly po-faced member of the village Garden Club faced with a technically demanding garden task. Consult Alice B. Toklas or Betsy Bell for the original recipe (Books for Cooks, London, kindly always keeps copies), but try sautéing the hemp buds in the very butter required by the recipe for best results.

Giant Hogweed *(Heracleum mantegazzianum)*

Also known as the cartwheel plant or giant cow parsnip, this stunning architectural plant, rising to three and a half metres in height, has sap that makes the skin hypersensitive to bright sunlight and therefore liable (certain) to blister and burn. It was dubbed 'The Triffid' (after John Wyndham's monster) in the 1970s by the press after several children were hospitalised by using the stalks as blow-pipes. It is the perfect gift for someone with eczema and/or irritating children. The added bonus is that the recipient could even get arrested if they were seen to be introducing it unchecked, as it is a notifiable plant at DEFRA.

Greater Duckweed *(Lemna polyrrhiza)*

This innocuous-looking plant, usually sold as a good oxygen-ator for ponds, will rapidly colonise all available space at the expense of any other plants and choke the water surface. An excellent present for someone with a dinky little pond for their expensive Koi carp collection.

Hemlock (*Conium maculatum*; Mother die, Woomlicks, Kexies)

The names say it all. This is the plant that could land you in jail for life, the A-list celebrity poison that dispatched Socrates. You will definitely need an alibi, and you would have to hate your victim very much indeed to subject him/her to a long, lingering death that takes in paralysis, respiratory failure, and a loss of consciousness only at the bitter end. Timing is important, as the intended victim could mistake the young leaves as parsley only early in the year.

Indian balsam (*Impatiens glandulifera*; Policeman's helmet)

Another one that could land your enemy in trouble with DEFRA, this incredibly pretty, exotic plant has escaped from gardens on to riverbanks, where, unless it is kept in check, it will travel like an express train. It has the alarming habit of exploding its seed heads, spreading them far and wide, but most effectively in water, which allows it to travel huge distances. The hooded pink flowers appear in mid-summer up to heights of one and a half metres. Give this to someone with a stream flowing through their garden and incredibly tidy gardening neighbours.

Japanese Knotweed *(Fallopia japonica)*

This exotic plant was introduced by the Victorians and thought to be very useful groundcover. It has now achieved the status of No.1 Horticultural Terrorist. The discovery of even the tiniest piece of root can halt the most prestigious building project, due to the plant's ability to go underground and then re-emerge triumphant through the most carefully laid tarmac. Desperate scientists and economists, who have calculated the obscene cost of trying to keep it in check with chemicals, are now turning to natural predators which they hope will do the job. Subterfuge would have to be the modus operandi here, as most people are aware of the unwelcome vigour of this plant. Dropping just a tiny bit on their compost heap should do the trick.

Kava Kava Root *(Piper methysticum)*

If your conditions are tired, bored and tense and the Best Kept Village Competition Committee is winding you up, I thoroughly recommend planting this gorgeous evergreen tropical shrub. It eventually reaches two and a half to three metres in height, thriving in moist, rich soil in a heated greenhouse, and is native to the Polynesian islands where, I discovered, it had been used by the islanders as a religious and visionary herb and as an aphrodisiac for as long as they could remember. They would part-chew the roots, blend the result with coconut milk and then ferment it. The delicious effects of consumption include calmed spinal activity with euphoric relaxation (fortunately without mental impairment) and even tingling in the genitalia for the lucky few. I think the efforts of cultivation and preparation are amply repaid by the delicious sight of inappropriate behaviour by an interfering, worthy, elder statesperson of your village. For recipes, see Alternative Nature's online herbal.

Monkshood *(Aconitum napellus)*

The most stunning, hooded, violet-blue flowers late in the summer provide a cool contrast to hot-headed *Helenium*, *Helianthus*, *Echinacea* and *Crocosmia* and also supply the most poison – from *every part*. Anecdotal evidence exists of people being hospitalised for merely daring to split this perennial without wearing gloves. Warriors used to tip their arrows with its juice to ensure death. John Gerard, writing in 1597, fortunately gives an antidote; this unsavoury balm consists of a powder made of crushed flies that have feasted on the plant. This is another one that requires a solid alibi and an expensive lawyer.

Mother-in-law's Tongue
(Sansevieria trifasciata)

An incredibly useful plant that produces a large dose of strychnine, which should numb the victim's member for a helpful period when discussing Christmas arrangements or childrearing. It is an evergreen, rhizomatous perennial with a rosette of five lance-shaped, stiff, fleshy leaves spanning one and a half metres, banded horizontally with pale green and yellow. Administer this in conjunction with mother-in-law's cushion, a fabulously painful, large member of the cactus family, and no one should be in any doubt who wears the trousers.

Russian Vine (*Fallopia baldschuanica,* Mile-a-minute Vine)

This very attractive scrambler will happily climb to 12 metres, adorned with fluffy white flowers aging pink in the summer and autumn. Donate this to tidy neighbours with a minuscule shed or decaying fence they wish to screen and they will be enraged by its robust health and mass of dead, tangled stems in the winter months and yet legally powerless to have it removed. It is guaranteed to provoke a bad incident of Boundary Rage.

Gardening Terms

Gardening Terms Illuminated

Algicide: NOT the murder of men/dogs called Algernon but chemicals that kill algae.

Batter: NOT a light and crispy deep-fried coating to fish and chips or an illegal method of restraining an errant spouse but the more or less oblique angle at which hedge sides should be cut.

Chafer: NOT the description of an ill-fitting thong but an insect which feeds on the foliage and underground plant organs of trees and shrubs.

Chelsea Chop: NOT Vidal Sassoon's five-point bob created during the 1960s for Christopher Lloyd but Lloyd's technique of cutting back certain plants during Chelsea Flower Show week in order to stagger flowering times.

Companion Planting: NOT gardening with your partner (or, better still, someone you actually like) but the practice of placing certain plants together to reduce pests and diseases.

Contact Action: NOT getting to 'third base' but the term applied to the process by which a chemical damages or kills an organism on contact.

Cultivar: NOT a raging cultural snob or someone whose friendship you have cultivated but a contraction of 'cultivated variety'.

Deadhead: NOT a possible adolescent expression for a narcotics user or a devotee of 'the Grateful Dead' but the action of removing dead flower heads to prevent seeding.

Exocarp: NOT a breed of Koi carp found in the River Exe but the outer layer of tissue in a fruit. Also known as **epicarp** (NOT a sick carp).

Feathered Maiden: NO burlesque involved, this is just a one-year-old tree with side shoots.

Gurrilla Gardening: NOT vegetable-growing terrorist groups or eco-terrorists who blow up suburban gardens that use peat-based compost but groups of people who meet to garden on distressed roundabouts and road verges in the dead of night. It has been suggested that they could start up a closet environmental anarchists' dating agency but, whatever the case, horticulturally sensitive drivers like myself welcome their activism.

Green Wood: NOT inexperienced erective function but live timber that has been felled and has not yet seasoned.

Gross Feeder: NOT Homer Simpson's ingestion style but an adjective describing a plant that requires nutrient-rich conditions to thrive.

Gymnosperm: NOT particularly athletic sperm but plants with naked or unprotected ovules and reproductive organs arranged in cones.

Harden Off: NOT yet another expression for self-abuse but the process of gradually acclimatising plants that have been raised inside to the outside before planting out.

Hard Landscaping: NOT landscaping that is difficult to execute or magazines about this subject found on the top shelf of the newsagents but the parts of your garden made up of hard materials like walls, paths and buildings.

Heave: NOT the result of an excessive night's drinking but the action of frost on soil, which causes it to lift, unearthing newly planted plants.

Hotbed: NOT your bed full to capacity with willing and ready talent but a method of raising plants on a bed of manure, thus providing bottom-heat (no spanking necessary) and promoting growth. The plants that most readily respond to such filthy treatment are usually Gross Feeders (*see* p. 76).

Hybrid Tea: NOT a weird, snooty single-estate beverage but a type of rose resulting from the crossing of two different varieties.

Irishman's Cuttings: NOT a comment on the marvellously reliable manhood of Ireland but shoots that develop of their own accord around the base of plants and have roots attached.

Leggy: NOT an attribute shared by your ideal partner but the stems of plants which do not receive enough light and so become etiolated in trying to reach it.

Maiden: NOT a lovely, innocent young woman but a tree in its first year after having been grafted on to a root-stock.

Maiden Whip: NO S&M here, just a one-year-old tree without side shoots.

Mamillate: NOT the very British habit of mating under the influence of Marmite but the horticultural adjective meaning nipple-shaped. It is still liable to provoke childish smutty remarks and general silliness in the less high-brow gardener (*see also* gymnosperm p. 77).

Nap: NOT a brief shut-eye but a lawn surface, especially one that is flattened to lie in one direction.

Offset: NOT a lousy set of tennis or a dodgy heirloom but a young plant reproduced asexually by the parent, usually at the base. Not something to try at home.

Peduncle: NOT the term used for a family member with a fondness for pretty young boys but a flower stalk either of a single flower or an inflorescence.

Pricking out: NOT the erective function of a healthy male but the spacing of seedlings which have their first true leaves.

Pot-bound: NOT a gardener with a debilitating marijuana habit but a plant that has been too long in its pot without being potted on (*see below*).

Pot on: NOT a marijuana addict who refuses to stop but the action of placing a plant in a bigger pot so that it has room to grow.

Puffy: NOT your eyes after a heavy night but a descriptive term used in relation to chalky soils that contain a great deal of organic matter.

Smut: NOT the journalism supplied by the *Daily Sport* but a fungal disease of onions caused by promiscuous behaviour in naughty insects.

Softwood Cutting: NOT another term for circumcision but a method of vegetative propagation in spring using new shoots of the parent plant that are almost fully developed and just beginning to harden.

Spit: NOT the uncivilised ejection of saliva but a spade or fork's depth of soil.

Stool: NOT a lavatorial result but the crown of a plant that is being used to produce propagation material.

Strobilus: NOT a type of disco light but a cone produced by conifers.

Summer Bedding: NOT sleeping *au naturel* but annual or biennial plants raised almost to maturity and then planted out for summer display.

Sward: NOT sword in the received pronunciation of the BBC *c*.1950 but an expanse of short grass.

Tamping: NOTHING to do with the female menstrual cycle but the process of firming or gently compacting the soil around a new plant.

Thallus: NOT a thong designed for a phallus but vegetative growth that has not developed distinct roots, shoots or leaves.

Thinning Out: NOT the inevitable follicular fall-out of middle age but the action of removing surplus seedlings to prevent overcrowding.

Truss: NOT a surgical appliance worn to support a hernia but a compact cluster of fruit or flowers at the end of a stem.

Whip and Tongue: NOT a sexual practice but a type of graft where the stock and scion are prepared with complementary notches.

Verticillium Wilt: IS a problem that can affect a wide range of species. Best to see your GP.

Terribly Useful Garden Techniques

Fruit-Tree Pruning

Garden reference books make this simple procedure deliberately complicated. Here are my failsafe, easy-to-follow rules, which even a gardening virgin can follow.

a) To transform a maiden whip (*see* Gardening Terms, p. 78) into a married standard, cut all the lower branches with a sloping cut of 45.5 degrees exactly at the second bud that presents its third outer wrapped leaflet to the moon on Wednesdays. This must be done between the hours of three and four on an afternoon when at least 23.2 hours of sunlight are forecast, and at *no* other time.

Note: 'Pixy' rootstock makes the cutest maidens.

b) To train a second-year feathered maiden (*see* Gardening Terms, p. 76) into a fan, start with the correct equipment:

   i) several goblets of the best available brandy to engender confidence so that, should the maiden protest, you don't take any notice

   ii) very sharp, expensive, *Swiss* secateurs, available only at the best horticultural emporium in downtown Basel

iii) a large, pristine wall facing south, most of the time studded artistically with Bulthaup brushed-steel hooks with stout canes attached

iv) acres of organic twine or silk ties made by either Armani or Versace, depending on the style to which you aspire

Then make sure you know which branch is the leader. To do this you need to advertise widely, making sure you do not discriminate on grounds of age, gender or disability. I tend to hire the best headhunter in the business. Competing leaders must be undercut with loppers so that they do not irritate the management team and, obviously, weeping standards must be swiftly eliminated following correct procedure.

Finally, make sure that your maiden is healthy, with a strong, uncongested frame and that she likes you a lot. Chocolates, champagne and tickets to the next Coldplay concert followed by a meal at a Ramsay restaurant are all very helpful. Then choose two laterals about 30 centimetres above the ground and masterfully cut these limbs to 40 centimetres and tie them to the canes on the wall at an angle of 40 degrees; savagely prune back all the other laterals to one happy bud. This does sound very aggressive, but no pain, no gain. It does look lovely and will produce heavy yields of fruit in a couple of years, provided you have not been sued first, if the maiden was not a real fan. In subsequent early summers you will need to keep tying in the leaders with index-linked benefits and pinch back other shoots on the maiden's ribs to one leaf to promote growth.

Success on the Show-bench

Making your own potting compost is the only way to guarantee super-sized plants for the show-bench. Recipes are a closely guarded secret in the horticultural industry, but the following should produce excellent results:

1 part home-made compost made from kitchen and garden waste plus cardboard turned homeopathically every fortnight

1 part cellulite (to bind all the nutrients together in a lumpy mass)

1 part horticultural sand dug by hand and imported from Norfolk

1 part sun-dried and smoked kelp from the Shetland Isles

1 part organic chicken manure, from the Buff Orpington breed only, graded and sieved after three years' rotation

Place all these ingredients in a heavy-bottomed terracotta flowerpot and bake, covered with greaseproof paper, in a very low oven for two months.

If this does not work, anabolic steroids can be used, as RHS Show organisers have not yet introduced on-the-spot drugs checks on plants or growers. Be sure to follow the correct dosage, as indicated on the packets, otherwise you may end up resembling your plant (just look at owners and their dogs).

Garden Design Dissected

Armed with my central organic philosophy and after many successful years of garden consultation and designing my own garden, I have developed some helpful guidelines for good design.

First, consider the overall structure of the garden. You must be *ruthless* and not allow sentiment of any kind to cloud your judgement. Friends cannot be relied upon to exercise taste in their horticultural gifts, and their ghastly plants must be dispatched to the compost immediately. The same applies to elderly shrubs and trees in the wrong places in your newly acquired garden. You must also decide how you wish to use your garden before putting in any permanent structures, such as paths and terraces, in order to save yourself costly errors. If you are unsure, acquire a handsome professional and make sure they understand your budget.

Another good tip is to try to engender a sense of place by inviting the wider landscape into your plot. You can use precise plants to indicate your locale, for example, *Clematis* 'Guernsey Cream' can be used in the Channel Isles and *Calluna vulgaris* 'Highland Rose' in Scotland, but do be careful about using towns, as they can look insufferably naff, especially *Chrysanthemum* 'Primrose West Bromwich'.

Maintenance issues are also an essential consideration before you finally decide on a particular garden style. Manicures, pedicures, aromatherapy massage and regular haircuts are all important for the gardener, and it is very difficult to find good-looking staff these days. A favourite tool of mine to give extended interest in the garden is the Chelsea Chop (*see* Gardening Terms, p. 75), created for guru Christopher Lloyd. Lloyd was much admired for his striking colour schemes, but this look is hated by the ladies-who-lunch in Chelsea. (Personally, I have found that sticking only to Farrow and Ball 'String' beiges has produced ravishing results for this type of client.) These ladies allow some contrasts, but they tend to be in more muted colours – *Iris sibirica* 'Marshmallow Frosting' looks pathetic with *Iris sibirica* 'Butter and Sugar' but fantastic with the dark brown foliage of Geranium *maculatum* 'Espresso' for the gourmet client of Notting Hill.

Use large groups of plants for maximum effect in a planting scheme and search for contrasting textures of flower and foliage. I personally find large groups of religious plants like *Dahlia* 'Bishop of LLandaff' rather fundamental-ist and much prefer *Eryngium alpinum* 'Superbum' among drifts of *Sisyrinchium* 'E. K. Balls' for more exciting year-round interest.

Planting styles you might like to consider include the following:

Restoration Gardening was effectively started by Graham Stuart Thomas when down-at-heel aristocratic families started to donate cripplingly expensive country houses to the fledgling National Trust after the two World Wars. The main idea was to remain faithful to the period by using only materials and plants available at the time of the garden's creation. For most of us lesser mortals, with less extensive means at our disposal, a brief consideration of historical accuracy is all you need to bother with. If, for example, you own a London residence of *c*.1780, why not try to incorporate the vast, flowing lines of Capability Brown, and a Ha-ha to separate you from the neighbours? After all, as Walpole observed, the genius William Kent 'leapt the garden and saw all nature was a fence'.

The Cottage Garden style is probably the nation's favourite, judging by the cooing response to re-creations of the Yorkshire Dales at RHS garden shows. It is a romantic brand recognised throughout the world, like Mills and Boon. Thatch cottages with tiny plots, intensively cosseted, are adorned with necklaces of lupins, foxgloves, ladies' mantle and roses. The problem is that few remain authentically rural and are now usually slap bang next door to an executive estate.

Classic Elegance sounds like one of the Bentley car models and definitely applies to the owners or aspiring owners of such a vehicle. This style combines some of the formality of your period pile — box-edged borders, lime hedges on stalks and bold topiary — along with a restrained use of favourite cottage plants. It is a totally *safe* option, though. So, for those of you for whom safety is death to the artistic soul, read on and pilfer ideas from some of the more modern options below.

Prairie Planting is inspired by wild meadows in the States, where it has become popular as a reaction against the imported 'English Garden'. It usually translates here as massed ranks of *Helenium*, *Rudbekia*, *Echinacea*, *Eupatorium* (i.e. American weeds) and various grasses planted *en masse*. I know some find the idea of 'planting' grasses at all anathema, but it can look superb in the autumn and winter. Just add lots of bulbs, and it could look fabulous for a suburban front garden, too, instead of it being a wretched parking facility.

European New Wave is typified by the vast textured grids of designer Piet Oudolf and uses prairie plants combined with perennials. Just make sure you do not have climbing frames, pools, terraces, buildings or cars in the way or they'll spoil the effect. Oudolf has also collaborated successfully with Minimalism and Conceptualism, who are great friends in the garden, as you can have a minimal idea as your concept. This usually translates as a large lump of hard landscaping, expensive lighting and gadgets such as a dance floor/cinema/water feature and few, if any, plants. Not much in it for the naturalistic gardener, but it is excellent if you need to flaunt modernist credentials and loads of cash. Top of the conceptual castle is the designer Martha Schwartz, whose use of bagels makes her easily confused with naughty culinary Martha Stewart.

Wild Gardening, also known as Habitat Parks or Natural Gardening, is a strong prevailing contemporary style. In Malmesbury, this means gardening in the nude, but that is only a local phenomenon. In general, this style is for those who enjoy a bit of rough in their garden and it attempts to make the garden look as untouched as possible. It requires very 'soft' hard landscaping (*see* Gardening Terms, p. 77), the use of lots of native plants (i.e. weeds), no straight lines or symmetrical clipped shapes, and habitats for wildlife, for example, piles of logs for frogs (i.e. mess). Many gardeners feel that it represents slovenly garden-keeping – the horticultural equivalent of Tracey Emin's *My Bed*. It is a difficult style to achieve, and an irritating side effect is that no one can tell if you have actually done any gardening. You may even have to learn the names of common weeds in Latin so that visitors realize your planting was deliberate.

I hope that this has given you a feel for some of the current themes in gardening. In my own modest acreage, I have plumped for a hybrid of these modern styles, even though my garden is best described as on the savage side of 'Wild'. This means, in practice, that only aromatherapy, occasional chiropractic treatment and herbal aphrodisiacs are strictly necessary as maintenance. This happens to suit my hectic life as a celebrity icon of garden style, fashionista and gourmet wife.

Appendix I:
My Perennial
Wardrobe

I feel very strongly that you must always look fabulous in the garden, as you never know who might show up, and it definitely will add style to your borders, especially in those tricky bits after the first spring flush but before summer roses and peonies start. You can just apply my new perfume *Effluence de Composte* to your person and the plants and plunge yourself into a wide section of the border. I suggest a good drinks supply, as you can often end up there for quite a while (*see* wine list in Appendix II, p. 95).

'Red Undies' *(Begonia)*
'Kashmir Blue' light sweater *(Geranium)*
'Purple Petticoats' *(Heuchera)*
'Claret Cloak' *(Vitis coignetiae)*, if it is cold
'Wide Brim' hat *(Hosta)*
Slipper Orchids

And for special occasions, try the elegant and
exclusive *Iris* 'Black Tie Affair'

You can find all these designs on-line at Plant-à-Porter by
going on to the RHS Plantfinder site (<u>rhs.org.uk</u>).

Appendix II:
Food in My Garden
(Flavum var. maximum)

I have been inspired to ever giddier heights due to the shining creative example of Heston Blumenthal. My chef, Gore May, and I have sweated to provide a cutting-edge horticultural menu, some of it traditional to this area of Dorset. To cut down on air miles and remain faithful to the spirit of my savage garden, I absolutely insist that nothing is eaten that comes from further than five metres from the house, and I personally often forage from my adjoining hedgerow. All ingredients are hand-pollinated in my garden where possible and picked only by attractive workers to avoid unnecessary stress to the plants. This has meant that I have kept well ahead of the Dorset cream-tea competition on Garden Open Days – my teas are not just scones, they are not just organic, they are unadorned natives.

Offered during my open garden tours at the following times:

5–5.30 p.m, winter Saturdays
4–4.15 a.m. last Wednesday in the summer months
Fees: £0.50 adults; £50.00 children and pensioners)

Set 'Flava' Menu of three courses

Price on demand, including coffee and *Begonia* 'Cocktail' with *Anemone hupehensis* 'Crispa'

1st Course:
Papaver orientale 'Watermelon'
or
sushi *Prunus* 'Kiku-shidare-zakura'

Main:
Rhododendron 'Woodcock' served with *Anthemis tinctoria* 'Sauce Hollandaise' and *Sedum spectabile* 'Iceberg' salad

Vegetarian option:
Vegetable Lamb with Tartary Sauce *(Cibotium barometz)*

Pudding:
Eupatorium rugosum 'Chocolate' tower with *Heuchera* 'Caramel' sauce, accompanied by *Ajuga reptans* 'Chocolate Chip' cookies.

Note:
We serve Hadspen rather than Wisley cream, as it is local. You can request *Helleborus orientalis* 'Harvington's Double Cream' in advance or *Kniphofia* 'Vanilla' ice cream.

Coffee:
single estate, fair-trade brand
Geranium maculatum 'Espresso'

Wine List:
Iris sibirica 'Sparkling Rosé'
a very pinky rosé with a blue tint to the flavour

Echinopsis 'Pink Champagne'
a fresh pink type with a yellowish-orange streak to the
middle of the flavour. Great in really hot weather.

Astrantia major 'Claret'
a rich red colour which can persist all summer

Penstemon 'Port Wine'
for the great-aunts in your party

Rosa 'Whisky Gill'
a gorgeous, fruity blend with a heady scent
and good apricot colour

Acknowledgements

I am delighted to acknowledge the unfailing, naughty support of the following: Aunt Suzie, the naughtiest of them all; Jonathan Papp, a close second, when he should have been practising; my mother and Giorgio; Ginny, who begged to read and amend the first draft; my husband and my children; Annabel, Damaris, Bella, Julia, Jules, Anouchka, Rory, Benita, Carol Klein, Bleddyn and Sue Wynn-Jones, Big Toby, Laetitia, Jenny, Kerenza, Tristan, Annie, Charlotte, Sarah, Robin Wallis and Susan Richards, who made me start.

Index

Aquilegia vulgaris var. *stellata* 'Nora
    Barlow' 54
Ajuga reptans 'Chocolate Chip' 94
Amorphophallus 13–14
Anemone hupehensis 'Crispa' 94
Anthemis tinctoria 'Sauce Hollandaise'
    94
Aster
  amellus 'King George' 50
  'Climax' 24
  ericoides 'Rosy Veil' 42
  novi-belgii 'Archbishop' 42
  oblongifolius 'Fanny's' 24
  Astilbe
  'Bumalda' 24
  'Gloria' 58
Astrantia major
  'Claret' 95
  'Sunningdale Variegated' 54
Author
  as celebrity icon 89
  fabulous wardrobe of 91–2
  horticultural abuse 9
  maintenance of 13, 89
  and totally organic cream teas 93
  worrying weaknesses of 53
Azalea (*Rhododendron*)
  'Adonis' 28
  'Queen Wilhelmina' 28
  'Willy' 28

Bastard
  Balm (*Melittis melissophyllum*) 14
  see also Rosa 'Playboy'
Begonia

'Cocktail' 94
'Red Undies' 14, 91
Bergenia 'Baby Doll' 62
Bishop's Weed (*Aegopodium
    podagraria*) 37–8
blackspot 47
Bum
  and bottom-heat 77
  Bum-pipe 24
  and Roman practice 17, 40
  sily 40
  'Superbum' 17

cactus 74
Calluna vulgaris 'Highland Rose' 85
Camellia
  Japonica 'Tiffany' 63
  x williamsii 'Bow Bells' 38
Campanula lactiflora 'Pouffe' 34
Campsis radicans 'Flamenco' 28–9
Cannabis sativa (Pot, Hash, Weed)
    69–70
Carex
  flagellifera 39
  stricta 39
Caryopteris x clandonensis 'Heavenly
    Blue' 38
Catholic church 16
  and Immaculate Conception 40
  and the Vatican 37
Ceanothus thyrsiflorus 'Borne Again'
    42
Cercis canadensis 'Forest Pansy' 29
Charles, HRH the Prince of Wales
  and companion planting 10

Charles, HRH – *cont.*
  and hosta 46
  see also Clematis
Chelsea Chop 75, 86
Chrysanthemum
  'Duchess of Edinburgh' 50
  'Primrose West Bromwich' 85
  x superbum 'Wirral Supreme' 54
Cibotium barometz 94
Clematis
  'Belle of Woking' 55
  'Duchess of Edinburgh' 47
  'Guernsey Cream' 85
  'Gypsy Queen' 55
  'Horn of Plenty' 14–15
  'Lemon Chiffon' 55
  montana 'Marjorie' 55
  montana 'Mayleen' 55
  'Prince Charles' 10, 47
'Princess Diana' 10, 29, 46–7
  'Ramona' 55
Clitoria
  location of 15
  and red spider mite 15
  see also Aster; Gynura; Magnolia;
    Malus; Narcissus; Pussy Willow
Cnicus, all types 15
  benedictus 15
Cock's Head (*Plantago lanceolata*)
  24
compost
  Effluence de Composte 91
  potting 83
contraception 14
Cotinus coggygria 'Royal Purple'
  50
Cox Apples 16
Crocosmia x crocosmiiflora
  'Lady Hamilton' 50
  'Zeal Tan' 62

Dahlia
  'Bishop of Llandaff 38, 86
  'Furka' 24
  'Gay Princess' 34
Debrett's Peerage 46
Delphinium 'Yvonne' 58
Dianthus
  'Doris' 58
  'Gran's Favourite' 29
Dicentra spectabilis 'Dutchman's
    Trousers' 16
doctor
  blood-pressure 9
  contraception 14
  control of disease 15, 16, 17, 18
  erectile disfunction 17, 23
  gout 37
  orchidectomy 20
  piles or wens in the flesh 21
  scrofula, 'the king's evil' 21
  syphilis 18
  ulcerous nipples 19
drink
  brandy as confidence-booster 81
  wine list 95
drugs
  anabolic steroids and the RHS
    83
  aphrodisiacs 20, 72, 89
  cannabis 69–70
  Kava Kava root 72–3
Dutchman's Trousers 16

Echinopsis 'Pink Champagne' 95
Emin, Tracey, bed of 89
Erigeron 'Quakeress' 39
Eryngium alpinum 'Superbum' 17,
    86
Eupatorium rugosum 'Chocolate'
    tower 94

Fagus sylvatica 'Pendula' 29–30
feathered maiden 76, 81
Festuca glauca 'Elijah Blue' (Blue fescue) 9, 39
fruit-tree pruning 81–2
Fuchsia
  'Phyllis' 58
  'Requiem' 42
  'Tracie Ann' 58

Galanthus 'Lady Beatrix Stanley' 50
Gaviscon 55
genitalia, tingling in 73
genome 27–8
Geranium
  'Kashmir blue' 91
  maculatum 'Espresso' 86, 95
  x oxonianum 'Lady Moore' 50
Geum
  'Lady Stratheden' 50
  'Mrs J. Bradshaw' 58
Giant Hogweed (*Heracleum mantegazzianum*), and irritating children 70
Ginkgo biloga 'Tit' 24
Greater Duckweed (*Lemna polyrrhiza*) 70
gymnosperm 77
Gynura 17

Hedera helix 'Erecta' (Common English ivy) 17
Heffner, Hugh 21
Helenium 'Chelsey' 62
Heliogabalus, Emperor 21
Helleborus
  hybridus 'Lady Charlotte Bonham-Carter' 50
  orientalis 'Harvington's Double Cream' 94

Hemerocallis
  'Anastasia' 63
  'Blonde is Beautiful' 65
  'Eighteen Carat' 65
  'Gay Rapture' 34
  'Little Bugger' 24
  'Lusty Leland' 24
  'Pardon Me' 55
  'Siloam Rose Queen' 50
  'Tonia Gay' 34
  'Twenty Third Psalm' 42
Hemlock (*Conium macultum*) 71
Heuchera
  americana 'Beauty Colour' 63
  'Caramel' sauce 94
  'Chocolate Ruffles' 58
  'Lady Romney' 50
  'Obsidian' 63
  'Purple Petticoats' 91
  'Red Spangles' 62–3
Hillier Manual of Trees and Shrubs 30, 31, 40
Hoary Allison (*Berteroa incana*) 18
Hosta
  'Big Daddy' 46
  'Royal Splendour' 46
  'Royal Standard' 46
  Stiletto' 65
  'Tattoo' 65
  'Wide Brim' hat 91
hybrid tea 77
Hydrangea sprrata 'Tiara' 65

Ilex x altaclerensis 'Golden King' 47–8
Indian balsam (*Impatiens glandulifera*) 71
Iris
  'Black Tie Affair' 92
  'Champagne Elegance' 46

Iris – cont.
  laevigata 'Regal' 50
  (Reticulata) 'Pauline' 58
    sibirica 'Butter and Sugar' 86
    'Harpswell Halleluja' 42
    'Marshmallow Frosting' 86
    'Sparkling Rosé' 95
    'Super Ego' 65
  spuria subs. musselmanica 34

Japanese Knotweed (*Fallopia japonica*), 72

Kava Kava Root (*Piper methysticum*)
The King Fern (*Dryopteris affinis* 'Cristata') 50
knickers 15

Lamium maculatum 'White Nancy' 34
Lathyrus 'Jet Set Group' 63
leggy 78
Lilium
  'Cheyenne' 63
  'Crystal Palace' 65
  'Destiny' 63
Linaria purpurea 'Canon J. Went' (Toadflax) 39
Lobelia
  cardinalis 40
  siphilitica 9, 18
  'Tania' 63
Lupinus
  'Aston Villa' 65
  'The Chataleine' 46

Magnolia
  'Heaven Scent' 42
  'Hot Lips' 24
  macrophylla 'Holy Grail' 40
  'Randy' 24

maiden 78
  feathered 76
  training 81
  whip 78, 81
Malus domestica
  'Brown Nose' 55
  'Golden Knob' 24
  'Lady's Finger' 24
  'Reverend W. Wilks' 42
  'Ten Commandments' 42
mamillate, Marmite 78
manure 77
Milk Thistle (*Silybum marianum*) 40
Miscanthus sinensis 'Gnome' 56
Monkshood (*Aconitum napellus*) 73
Morning Glory (*e.g. Ipomoea hederacea*) 18
Mother die *see* Hemlock (*Conium macultum*)
Mother-in-law's Cushion 74
Mother-in-law's Tongue (*Sansevieria trifasciata*), 73–4

Naked
  Boys, Ladies, Nannies, Virgins (*Colchium autumnale*) 24
nap 78
Narcissus 'Canaliculatus' 19
naturist 20
nipple
  ulcers of 19
Nipplewort (*lapsana communis*) 19
nuts 30
Nymphaea 'Pink Starlet' 65

orchids
  Early-purple (Male orchid, Sweet ballocks, Dog-stones) 19–20

Slipper 91
Oudolf, Piet 88

Paeonia lactiflora
  'Barrymore' 58
  'Duchesse de Nemours' 50
Papaver orientale
  'Brooklyn' 63
  'Watermelon' 94
Pelargonium 'Romeo' 63
Pemberton, Reverend Joseph 41
penis 23
Penstemon
  'Port Wine' 95
  whippleanus 34
phallus plants *see Amorphophallus*;
    Hedera helix; Morning Glory;
    Prunus; Sticky Willy;
    Trachelospermum; Welsh Dicks;
    Willy Lily
Phlox adsurgens 'Red Buttes' 24
Phormium
  'Apricot Queen' 30
  'Rainbow Queen' 30
Phygelius x rectus 'African Queen' 30
Pixy rootstock 81
Potentilla
  fruticosa 'Chelsea Star' 65
  thurberi 'Monarch's Velvet' 50
Primula allioni 'Mary Berry' 54
Priscilla, Queen of the Desert (film)
    30
promiscuous
  as irreverent coupling 27
  as rampant seeding 27
Prunus
  domestica 'Warwickshire Drooper'
    24
  'Kiku-shidare-zakura' 94
Pussy Willow (*Salix caprea*) 24

red spider mite 15
Red Undies 14, 91
reproduction 13–14, 15, 17, 40
Rhododendron
  Azalea 'Adonis'
  'Faggetter's Favourite' 31
  'Kokinshita' 31
  vernicosum 'McLaren T71' 65
  'Woodcock' 94
Romans
  emphasis on bum 17
  medicine against gout 37
  propaganda 40
Rosa
  'Bobby charlton' 64
  'Buff Beauty' 20
  'Camp David' 31–2
  'Cardinal Hume' 40
  'Celebrity' 64
  'Champagne Cocktail' 65
  'Climbing Fashion' 65
  'Dolly Parton' 32
  'Duftwolke' 32
  'The Fairy' 32–3
  'Fame' 64
  'Felicia' 41
  'The Friar' 42
  'La Reine' 34
  'Lady Mary Fitzwilliam' 45
  'Lady Gay' 32
  'Lady Hillingdon' 49
  'Lady Waterlow' 45
  'Lagerfeld' 34
  'Ma Perkins' 41
  'Madame Pierre Oger' 41
  'Mother's Day' 29
  'Mrs Honey Dyson' 56
  'Nathalie Nypels' 20
  'Oklahoma' 32
  'Paul Crampel' 32

Rosa – cont.
  'Playboy' 21
  'Princess of Wales' 47
  'The Prioress' 41
  'Pur Caprice' 65
  'Queen of Denmark' 46, 50
  'The Queen Elizabeth' 48
  'Queen Mother' 48
  'Sunseeker' 65
  'Super Star 64
  'Weightwatcher's Success' 65
  'Wembley Stadium' 65
  'Whisky' 95
Rosemarinus prostratus 39
Royal Horticultural Society (RHS)
Russian Vine (*Fallopia baldschuanica*)
    74

Salvia var. *turkestanica* 'Sweaty Typist'
    7
Scrophularia nodosa (Knotted figwort,
    Throatwort) 21–2
Sedum spectabile 'Iceberg' salad 94
Sisyrinchium 'E.K. Balls' 22, 86
spit 79
Sticky Willy (*Galium aparine*) 22
strobilus 79

tamping 80
testicles 20
Trachelospermum 33
Tulipa

'Abba' 56
'Angelique' 57
clusiana 'Cynthia' 57
'Maureen' 56
'Monte Carlo' 65
'Shirley' 56
'Wendy Love' 56

undies *see Begonia*; *Cnicus*

Verbascum 'Jackie' 58
Verticillium wilt 80
vice
  deviant hybrids 31
Viola
  cazorlensis 'Colleen' 65
  tricolor (Wild pansy) 34
Virgin 40
Vitis coignetiae 'Claret Cloak' 91

weeds
  American 88
  Latin names 89
  organic 9
Welsh Dicks (*Salix purpurea*) 24
whip and tongue 80
whitefly 15
Willy Lily (*Arum maculatum*) 23

Yucca flaccida 'Golden Sword' 34

Zantedeschia 'Kiwi Blush' 58